Teach Me Christian Virtues
(grades 4-6)

by
Hollice H. Looney

Illustrated by
Darcy Tom

SELF-DISCIPLINE
COMPASSION
RESPONSIBILITY
COURAGE
PERSEVERENCE
LOYALTY
AND
FAITH

Cover by Tom Sjoerdsma

Copyright © 1996, Shining Star
A publication of Silver Burdett Ginn Religion Division

ISBN No. 0-382-30732-1

Standardized Subject Code TA ac

Printing No. 987654321

Shining Star Publications
1204 Buchanan St., Box 399
Carthage, IL 62321-0399

Unless otherwise indicated, the New International Version of the Bible was used in preparing the activities in this book.

Table of Contents

Self-Discipline 3

What Is Self-Discipline? 4

How Do You Spend Your Time? 5

How Should We Act? 6

Compassion 7

What Is Compassion? 8

What Can I Do? 9

People of Compassion 10

Responsibility 11

What Does It Mean to Be Responsible? 12

Responsible Words 13

What Is Your "Responsibility Quotient"? 14

Courage 15

What Do I Need When I Am Afraid? 16

Name Your Fear 17

The Meaning of Courage 18

Perseverance 19

The Meaning of Perseverance 20

Something to Struggle With 21

Signs for Perseverance 22

Loyalty 23

A Skytale for Loyalty 24

Secret Loyalty Puzzle 25

How Do You Show Your Loyalty? 26

Faith 27

What Is Faith? 28

Who Do People Say That I Am? 29

Living Our Faith 30

Answer Key 31

Self-Discipline

Children need to develop self-discipline as they grow. When they are small, discipline comes from other people. As they grow, we need to give them opportunities to practice self-discipline. Little by little, they will be able to handle more challenging situations.

Activity Pages

What Is Self-Discipline? page 4

To discover what self-discipline is, find a path through the puzzle. If children use highlighters, light colored crayons, or colored pencils to mark their way along the path, they will still be able to read the words under the path. Discuss how God helps us learn discipline and gives us self-control when we trust Him.

How Do You Spend Your Time? page 5

This activity should be done over a week's time. It is best if your students can list their activities at the end of each day while the things they have done are still fresh in their minds. If this is not possible, they could write, at one sitting, about the previous week. When students look at their schedule and analyze it, they should look carefully for ways they developed their minds, their bodies (sports, exercise, etc.), and gifts or talents they have. Did they have any quiet time for reading and reflection? Everyone needs downtime to relax and refresh the mind and body. What may look like wasted time may actually be necessary. What students should look for are excessive amounts of wasted time. Discuss how the students benefit from spending time in prayer and Bible reading.

How Should We Act? page 6

After students complete the activity, discuss what it means to humble oneself. Have your students give practical suggestions, such as giving someone else first choice.

Shining Star Publications, Copyright © 1996
0-382-30732-1

What Is Self-Discipline?

Find a path in the puzzle to discover what self-discipline is. Work carefully because there are many turns in this path.

END

BEGIN

WHO WILL
HELP YOU
DO THIS?

4

0-382-30732-1

How Do You Spend Your Time?

Complete this page during the next week. At the end of each day, write down what you have done. Try to remember everything!

Sunday	
Monday	
Tuesday	
Wednesday	
Thursday	
Friday	
Saturday	

After the week is over, circle all the activities that helped to develop your self-discipline. Draw a line through the activities that seemed to be a waste of time.

Can you think of some better ways to spend your time? How much time did you spend reading your Bible? Praying?

0-382-30732-1

How Should We Act?

Self-discipline means that we control ourselves. This includes controlling our pride. Read Luke 14:7-11. Solve the puzzle to find the meaning of this Bible story. Look at the key. Notice that the only area of the grid that looks like this ⌐_ is the ABC box. When one dot is placed in the bracket, choose the first letter in the box; two dots mean the second letter; and three dots mean the third letter.

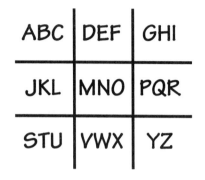

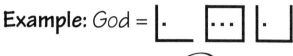

_____ _____ _____

_____ _____ _____

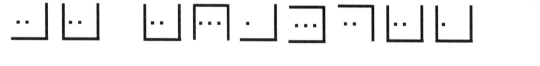

_____ _____ _____ ___. Luke 14:11b

What does this say to you about how you should act?

0-382-30732-1

Compassion

It is natural for children to be self-centered, particularly when they are young. As they grow, we need to direct them toward seeing others' needs and helping them. This will help our children become more "other-centered" and less self-centered. As they become aware of other people and learn to care about their needs, their compassion will grow.

Activity Pages

What Is Compassion? page 8

After students complete this activity page, talk about the best example of a compassionate person—Jesus. Ask students to recall some ways Jesus showed compassion (healing people, forgiving them, raising the dead, etc.). If they need help remembering specific stories, have them look over Mark 5-9.

What Can I Do? page 9

After your children find all the words in the puzzle, have them mention other gifts and abilities. List these on the board. Ask the children to decide how they can use their gifts and abilities to show compassion to other people. Encourage them to be specific. (Example: A boy who is good at storytelling can entertain a young brother or sister when his mother isn't feeling well.) Pray the following prayer as a group:

Heavenly Father, I thank You
For all the things that I can do.
I'll use my talents to follow Your plan
And be of help wherever I can.

People of Compassion, page 10

Be sure to point out to your children that only the large dots are used in this Braille activity. If you have access to a Braille typewriter, you might want to type the coded message out and let them feel it. This will help them see how a blind person can "read" with his fingers.

0-382-30732-1

What Is Compassion?

Change the spacing between the "words" below to find an important message about compassion.

TH EREAR ET WOPA R TSTO

COM PAS SIO N:CAR I NGA ND

DO IN GSO METH INGT OSH OW

THATY OUCA RE.

_____

_____

_____

What does this mean for you?

0-382-30732-1

What Can I Do?

God gives us gifts and abilities to use for Him. Circle the eighteen words that are hidden in the puzzle. Words appear forward, backward, and diagonally.

```
R S A B S M I L E C I S P
A O T M U R R F O M S C R
T H M O M R K O A E L R A
H E J U R R K G H T O E Y
L L L B H Y I C O O G A E
E P W Z A N T E L Q I T R
T F S R A Y S E U B C I F
I U T T C J B M L T A V U
C L I I P E R Z A L L E L
O O S G N I D A E R I A C
N U L A U G H T E R T N C
M C V G N I N E D R A G G
Z H Q C I T E M H T I R A
```

ARITHMETIC	GARDENING	MUSIC
ART	HELPFUL	PRAYERFUL
ATHLETIC	HUMOR	READING
CHESS	IMAGINATION	SMART
COOK	LAUGHTER	SMILE
CREATIVE	LOGICAL	STORYTELLING

Which of these gifts and abilities do you have? Can you think of others you have? Can you think of someone who may need your help? How can you use your gift or talent to show compassion for that person?

0-382-30732-1

People of Compassion

Complete the Bible verse by matching the Braille symbol in the words below with the letter in the key. Write the letter in the space below the symbol. **Note:** Only the large dots are used. Read Colossians 3:12 to check your answer:

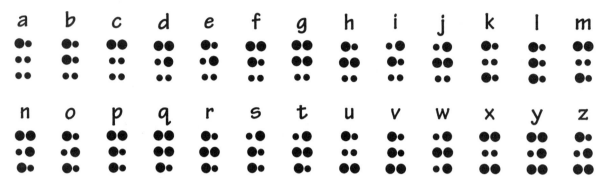

"Therefore, as God's chosen people, holy and dearly loved, clothe yourselves with

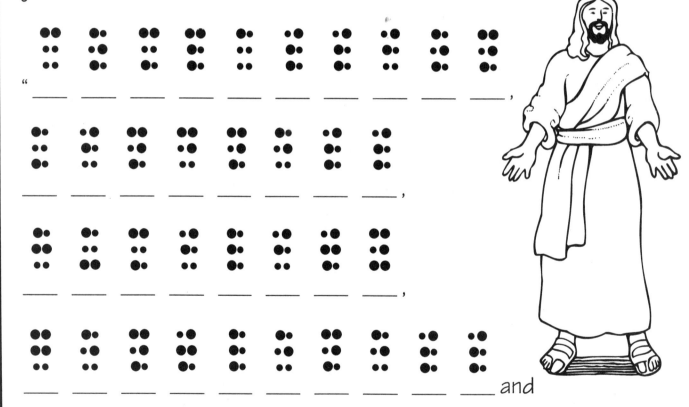

What do you think this verse means? Is there someone who needs your help or care?

Responsibility

Children need to be challenged to be responsible. When they are young, we expect them to be responsible for small things or in very specific areas. As they mature, our expectations for them grow along with their understanding of responsibility. The story of Joseph in Genesis 39-41 is an excellent example of being responsible, no matter what the situation. You may want to tell your students a brief version of this story.

Activity Pages

What Does It Mean to Be Responsible? page 12

Have students complete this page first in small groups, then share it with the larger group. Discuss what it means to be a responsible Christian (Bible reading, prayer, doing right, etc.).

Responsible Words, page 13

You may want to give your students the first letter of each word as a clue. Discuss the practical meaning of each word. Talk about Romans 14:12.

What Is Your "Responsibility Quotient"? page 14

The statements on this page identify some key concepts of responsibility about which your students should think. Encourage them to respond honestly to each statement. Point out that God will help them be more responsible if they will trust Him.

If time permits, help students make a chart of responsibilities to take home to remind them to be responsible.

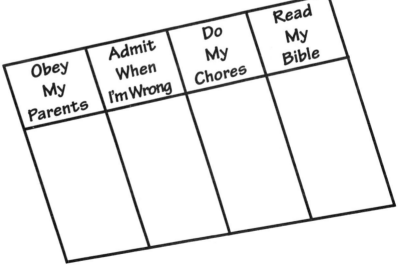

Obey My Parents	Admit When I'm Wrong	Do My Chores	Read My Bible

What Does It Mean to Be Responsible?

Hold this page up to a mirror to discover the meaning of responsibility.

If I am responsible, I know the difference between right and wrong and can think and act logically. That means that I answer for what I do.

Read Galatians 6:4 to see what God says about being responsible. How well do you do this?

0-382-30732-1

Responsible Words

Unscramble the following words about responsibility. Do you know what each one means? If not, look in a dictionary.

baelleir   __ __ l __ __ bl __

ucbanlcteoa   __ cc __ __ __ __ __ bl __

awnesr   __ __ sw __ __

lleiba   __ ia __ __ __

twrhrsotyut   __ __ __ st __ __ rt __ __

pdealenbde   d __ __ e __ __ __ bl __

afhlifut   __ ai __ __ __ __ __

llayo   l __ __ __ l

Read Romans 14:12. Do you ever try to blame someone else when you do wrong? God says He holds each one of us responsible for our actions!

What Is Your "Responsibility Quotient"?

For each of the questions or statements below, place a mark on the scale where you think you are at this time in your life.

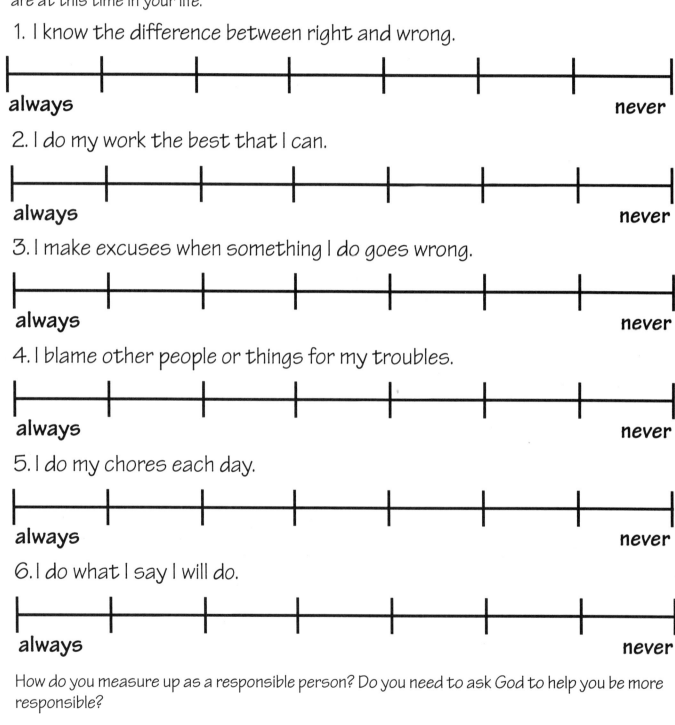

1. I know the difference between right and wrong.

always   never

2. I do my work the best that I can.

always   never

3. I make excuses when something I do goes wrong.

always   never

4. I blame other people or things for my troubles.

always   never

5. I do my chores each day.

always   never

6. I do what I say I will do.

always   never

How do you measure up as a responsible person? Do you need to ask God to help you be more responsible?

Shining Star Publications, Copyright © 1996

0-382-30732-1

Courage

We need to help our children realize that courage is how we deal with our fears. We are all afraid of something, whether we want to admit it or not. Facing our fears and acting as we should is how we show courage. There are times when we should stand and face our fears and there are times we should walk away. It takes experience and wisdom to know when to do either.

Activity Pages

What Do I Need When I Am Afraid? page 16

Your students may need help with this activity. If so, do it together as a group. Talk about God's promises to be with us in Isaiah 41:10 and other Bible verses, such as Psalms 34:4; 56:3-4; Mark 5:36b; John 16:33.

Name Your Fear, page 17

Part of being courageous is knowing about your fears. This puzzle helps students identify fears. Once we have identified our fears, we can begin to confront them. There will be many more fears than those listed as part of the crossword puzzle. Be careful that no one is made fun of because of a particular fear. Share some of your own fears and explain how you deal with them. Emphasize the importance of talking to God about your fears and trusting Him.

The Meaning of Courage, page 18

Facing our fears isn't easy for any of us. Remembering that God is with us helps a lot. Review the story of David and Goliath, 1 Samuel 17. Why was David brave enough to face a giant? Have students read 1 Samuel 17:37,45 to find the answer.

0-382-30732-1

What Do I Need When I Am Afraid?

If you follow the directions well, you will be able to discover what we need when we have fears and are afraid. Read each step carefully and do what it says.

1. Write the word <u>fears</u>. _____

2. Add <u>some</u> at the front. _____

3. Add a <u>u</u> after the 3rd letter. _____

4. Add a <u>cg</u> after the 8th letter. _____

5. Switch the 1st and 9th letters. _____

6. Drop the 7th, 9th, and 12th letters. _____

7. Switch the 5th and 9th letters. _____

8. Drop the 3rd and 6th letters. _____

This is what God promises to give us when we are afraid. Read Isaiah 41:10. God gives us courage by promising to be with us and help us.

Name Your Fear

Complete the puzzle with some fears we may have.

CLUES

Across

1. People swim in this.
3. Opposite of light
5. If you're afraid of these, don't go mountain climbing.
7. People your age
8. Some people think these haunt houses!
11. Creepy, crawly 8-legged creatures

Down

2. These have rain, lightning, and thunder.
3. These include German shepherds.
4. If you are afraid of these, you want to be alone.
6. Where you go to learn
9. Talking in front of a group of people
10. Smoke detectors warn us of this.
11. These reptiles can be harmful.

What else are you afraid of? Have you asked God to help you overcome your fear?

0-382-30732-1

The Meaning of Courage

To find out the meaning of courage, cut out the box below. Punch holes in the nine white squares. Place the box with the three white squares on top of the letters at the right. Match the corners of the box with the markers at the corners of the puzzle. The first nine letters of the message are visible from the left to right, top to bottom. Write them on the lines. Turn the box so the three white squares are on the right. Write the letters you see, left to right, top to bottom. Turn the box again so the three white squares are on the bottom. Copy letters you see in the same order. Turn the box once more so the three white squares are on the left. Copy the letters you see, and you have an explanation of courage.

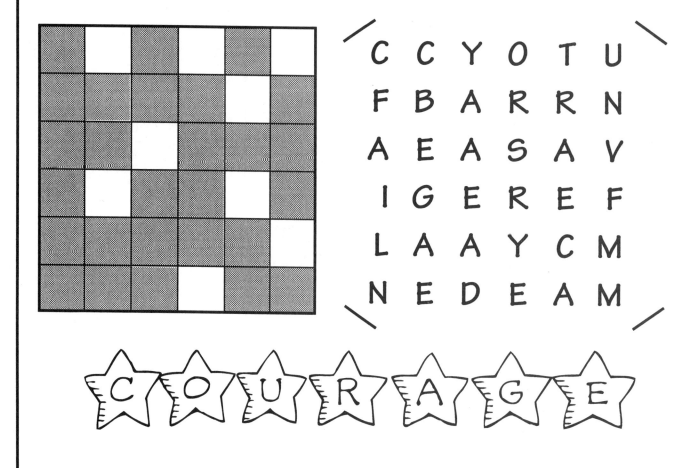

C C Y O T U
F B A R R N
A E A S A V
I G E R E F
L A A Y C M
N E D E A M

COURAGE

_____

_____

_____

Shining Star Publications, Copyright © 1996

0-382-30732-1

Perseverance

It is easy to become discouraged when we fail and to give up and say that we can't do something. That's the easy way out. We can also keep trying and learning from the mistakes we make. We become better people by trying again and, perhaps, accomplishing the task we set out to do. "If at first you don't succeed, try, try again."

Activity Pages

The Meaning of Perseverance, page 20

The secret message of this puzzle consists of every third letter. Instead of drawing a circle around every third letter, children may wish to underline it. Discuss John 8:31.

Something to Struggle With, page 21

The purpose of this activity is to think about the things we find difficult. How do we deal with them? Do we keep trying, or do we walk away? It may help your students to know that adults (parents and grandparents) struggle too. This could be a meaningful opportunity for sharing between generations as your students, parents, and possibly grandparents discuss difficult things and how they struggle with them.

Another good example of perseverance is Isaac in Genesis 26:12-22. In spite of being mistreated and taken advantage of by his neighbors, Isaac patiently persevered and God blessed him for it.

Signs for Perseverance, page 22

The hand signs are American Sign Language. After they complete this activity, let students try to sign the words. Discuss 2 Thessalonians 3:13b. Ask students to share their ideas about when they might get tired of doing right (when others make fun of them for doing right, when no one notices or rewards them, or when everyone else seems to be doing wrong and getting away with it). Remind them that God sees them doing right and will reward them someday.

0-382-30732-1

The Meaning of Perseverance

Circle every third letter in the letters below. Then copy the circled letters in order on the lines below. You will discover the meaning of perseverance.

ZXPCVEBNRMASSDEFGVHJEKLRQWAERNTYCUIEOPMZXECVABN
NMASSDTFGOHJKLQEWEERTPYUGIOOPZIXCNVBGNMEASVD
FEGHNJKILQFWEWRTEYUFIOAPOIIULYTARENWQDLKTJHOGFCD
SOAMNNBTVCIXZNQAUWSEEDIRFNTGSYHPUJIIKTOLEZAOXMFCD
DVFIBGFNHFMJIKICLOUAWLSETDRIFTEGYSHUOHURJIOKOBLP
SZSTXDACFCVGLBHENHS

Read John 8:31. What do you think it means to continue (persevere) in God's Word?

0-382-30732-1

Something to Struggle With

Perseverance has a lot to do with struggling—failing and trying again. Sometimes we must try many times. Complete the following sentences to show where you need perseverance.

Something that I find easy is _____

_____

_____.

Something that I find difficult is _____

_____

_____.

This is how I deal with this difficulty: _____

_____

_____.

Ask your parents or grandparents about something they struggle with. What is it? _____

_____.

How do they deal with the difficulty?_____

_____.

What can you learn from your parents or grandparents about perseverance and struggling with difficulty?
Read 2 Timothy 2:1,3 to see what God says about not giving up when things get tough.

0-382-30732-1

Signs for Perseverance

Use sign language to discover five other words or phrases that mean to persevere.

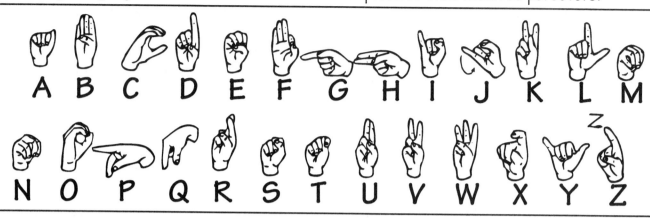

_____

_____

_____

_____

Can you make these hand motions to sign the words? Try signing part of a Bible verse about perseverance, 2 Thessalonians 3:13b.

0-382-30732

Loyalty

When we teach children about loyalty we are challenging them to become "other-centered." They should think about other people instead of themselves and show this in the way they act. Simply thinking about other people is not enough. Thought must be followed by actions. To illustrate loyalty, lead your students in a study of Jesus' disciples. Were they all loyal to Him? When did they show disloyal tendencies? When did they exhibit great loyalty, even after He was gone?

Activity Pages

A Skytale for Loyalty, page 24

This type of puzzle comes from ancient Greece, about 2400 years ago. A narrow piece of paper is wrapped around a cylinder; then a message is written on the strip of paper. When the paper is removed from the cylinder, the message cannot be read. The people sending and receiving the message must use the same size cylinder to read the message. Be sure when the strips of paper are put together that they do not overlap.

Secret Loyalty Puzzle, page 25

The purpose of this puzzle is to reinforce the idea that often loyalty calls for action from us. Discuss the kinds of actions that show loyalty to God, to friends, to the truth. Encourage children to be specific. (Examples: Not going along with the crowd to do wrong shows loyalty to God. Sticking up for a friend when someone else makes fun of him shows loyalty.)

How Do You Show Your Loyalty? page 26

Groups to which students belong might include family, scouts, sports teams, Sunday school class, etc. Once they have identified the groups, students should think about how they show their loyalty. Answers may be as simple as attending meetings, being at practice, paying attention. Is there something they should be doing to demonstrate their loyalty to a person or group that they are not currently doing? Students may need help coming up with ideas.

A Skytale for Loyalty

1	4	2	5	3	6
L	A	O	L	Y	T
Y	A	M	N	E	S
T	E	O	F	B	A
I	F	T	U	H	L
T	P	O	E	A	R
S	C	O	O	N,	U
N	Y,	T	C	R	A
U	O	S	R	E	
D	Y	U		T	

A skytale is a cylinder or tube around which a person can wrap a strip of paper in a spiral; then a message may be written on the paper. The message cannot be read when the paper is unwrapped because the letters are scrambled.

Cut out the strips of paper on the left. Tape the bottom of strip 1 to the top of strip 2 (with no overlap). Continue taping the bottom of each strip to the top of the next until all are together. Wrap the strip around a 12 ounce soda pop can in a spiral to read the secret message.

King David prayed that his people would be loyal to God. Read part of his prayer in 1 Chronicles 29:17-18. Are you loyal to the Lord?

Secret Loyalty Puzzle

Decode the letters to discover a special message about loyalty.

✿ = A ✳ = B ▲ = C ❖ = D ✡ = E

● = F ✛ = G ♣ = H ✪ = I ▢ = J

Ø = K ★ = L ✳ = M √ = N ◯ = O

| = P ✛ = Q ✺ = R ☆ = S ✻ = T

◗ = U ■ = V ✸ = W ▼ = X ☆ = Y

✪ = Z

— — — — — — — — — — — — — —

— — — — — — — — — — — — —

— — — — — — —

— — — — — — — — — — —

— — — — — — — — — — .

<u>Faithfulness</u> is a Bible word that is similar to <u>loyalty</u>. Read 3 John 3 to find out what Christians need to be faithful or loyal to.

0-382-30732-1

How Do You Show Your Loyalty?

What groups do you belong to? List them in the circles on the left. (Groups may include your family, clubs you belong to, teams you're on, and church groups.) How do you show loyalty to each group? Explain in the circles on the right.

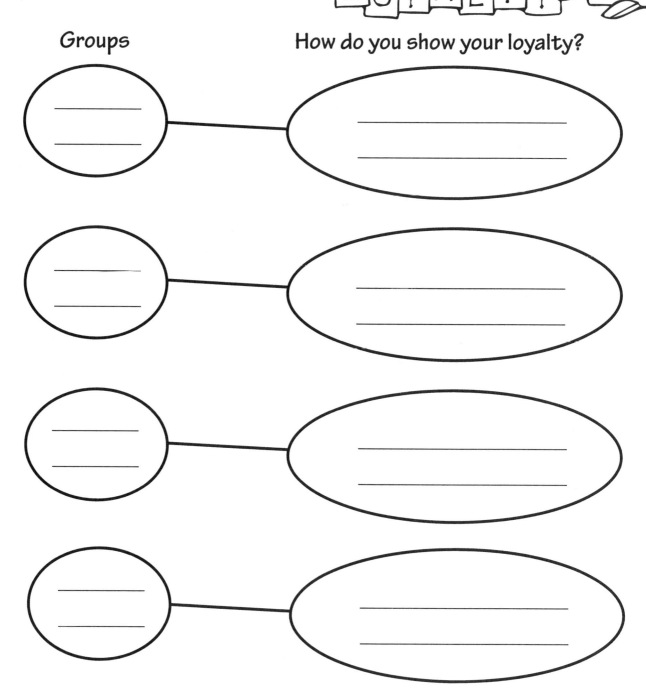

Groups

How do you show your loyalty?

Who should have your greatest loyalty? Why? Read Joshua 24:14a.

0-382-3073

Faith

Faith is believing in what we cannot see or prove. It influences what we do, how we act, what we believe, and how we live. Faith in God is simple for young children, but fourth to sixth graders are beginning to question and want proof. Encourage them to ask questions so you can find the answers together in God's Word. Share your own faith with them also.

Activity Pages

What Is Faith? page 28

After students complete the activity, talk about faith. Read through Hebrews 11. Talk about the Bible people mentioned, recalling how their faith was outstanding. Pick out two or three people, such as Noah, Joseph, Moses, with whom your students are familiar. Discuss how they demonstrated faith.

Who Do People Say That I Am? page 29

It takes faith to believe in Jesus. The Bible tells us all about Him, but how do we know we can believe the Bible? That takes faith too. Ask children what they believe about Jesus. Then ask them to consider <u>why</u> they believe. Because that's what their parents have taught them? Because that's what their friends believe? Because they have faith in God?

Living Our Faith, page 30

After students complete the activity, talk about the need to demonstrate our faith by our actions. It's easy to say, "I believe." It's much more difficult to prove that belief by what we do. The people mentioned in Hebrews 11 all proved their faith. Some of them suffered for it. But God rewarded them all. Ask students to think of ways they can prove their faith in God every day at home, school, and church. List their ideas on the board.

Why do I believe?

ining Star Publications, Copyright © 1996 0-382-30732-1

What Is Faith?

Use the telephone touch-tone buttons to decode the message about faith. Read Hebrews 11:1 to check your answer.

Example: 7 = P; 2 = B

> Pssst...
> HELP ME DECODE THE MESSAGE...

1	ABC 2	DEF 3
GHI 4	JKL 5	MNO 6
PRS 7	TUV 8	WXY 9
*	QZ 0	#

6 6 9 3 2 4 8 4   4 7

__ __ __ __ __   __ __ __ __ __

2 3 4 6 4   7 8 7 3 6 3

__ __ __ __ __   __ __ __ __ __ __

9 4 2 8   9 3   4 6 7 3

__ __ __ __   __ __   __ __ __ __

3 6 7   2 6 3   2 3 7 8   2 4 6

__ __ __   __ __ __   __ __ __ __   __ __ __

6 3 9   4 2 8   9 3   3 6

__ __ __   __ __ __   __ __   __ __

6 6 8   7 3 3

__ __ __   __ __ __ .

0-382-3073

Who Do People Say That I Am?

Jesus was called by different names. Cover the grid with a blank sheet of paper. Slowly slide the paper down until the first dot can be seen. Write the letter at the top of that line on the line below. Continue until you have finished the puzzle and have one of Jesus' names.

A B C D E F G H I J K L M N O P Q R S T U V W X Y Z

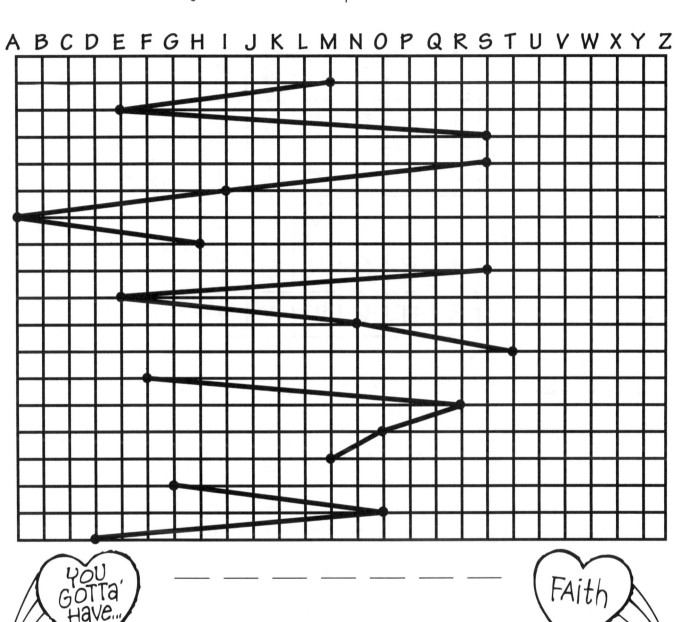

YOU GOTTA' Have...

FAith

___ ___ ___ ___ ___

___ ___ ___ ___ ___ ___

___ ___ ___ ___

Who do YOU say Jesus is? Do you have faith that He is who He said He is? Following Jesus takes faith.

0-382-30732-1

Living Our Faith

Solve the message below to find out what God says about faith in our everyday lives. Use the number/letter box to decode the message. Find the first digit of each number in the left column of the box and the second digit in the top row. Use the letter that intersects the two. Example: 15 = E   Read James 2:17b to check your answer.

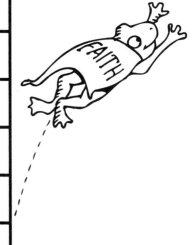

A leap of faith...

	1	2	3	4	5
1	A	B	C	D	E
2	F	G	H	I	J
3	K	L	M	N	O
4	P	Q	R	S	T
5	U	V	W	X	Y

21 11 24 45 23   12 55   24 45 44 15 32 21

" __ __ __ __ __   __ __   __ __ __ __ __ __ ,

24 21   24 45   24 44   34 35 45

__ __   __ __   __ __   __ __ __

11 13 13 35 33 41 11   34 24 15 14   12 55

__ __ __ __ __ __ __   __ __ __ __   __ __

11 13 45 24 35 34   24 44   14 15 11 14

__ __ __ __ __ __   __ __   __ __ __ __ ."

0-382-30732-

Answer Key

SELF-DISCIPLINE

What Is Self-Discipline? page 4
Self-discipline means to take control of myself and to develop myself into the person that God calls me to be. I will be happier and healthier if I can do this.

How Should We Act? page 6
He who humbles himself will be exalted.

COMPASSION

What Is Compassion? page 8
There are two parts to compassion: caring and doing something to show that you care.

What Can I Do? page 9

People of Compassion, page 10
compassion, kindness, humility, gentleness, patience

RESPONSIBILITY

What Does It Mean to Be Responsible? page 12
If I am responsible, I know the difference between right and wrong and can think and act logically. That means that I answer for what I do.

Responsible Words, page 13
reliable, accountable, answer, liable, trustworthy, dependable, faithful, loyal

COURAGE

What Do I Need When I Am Afraid? page 16
FEARS, SOMEFEARS, SOMUEFEARS, SOMUEFEACGRS, COMUEFEASGRS, COMUEFAGR, COMURFAGE, COURAGE

hining Star Publications, Copyright © 1996

0-382-30732-1

Name Your Fear, page 17

The Meaning of Courage, page 18
Courage means I face my fear and act bravely.

PERSEVERANCE

The Meaning of Perseverance, page 20
Perseverance means to keep going, even if we fail, and to continue in spite of difficulties or obstacles.

Signs for Perseverance, page 22
persist, endure, carry on, keep on, continue

LOYALTY

A Skytale for Loyalty, page 24
Loyalty means to be faithful to a person, country, cause, or duty.

Secret Loyalty Puzzle, page 25
To be loyal often means we should be doing something for someone else.

FAITH

What Is Faith? page 28
"Now faith is being sure of what we hope for and certain of what we do not see."

Who Do People Say That I Am? page 29
Messiah sent from God

Living Our Faith, page 30
"Faith by itself, if it is not accompanied by action, is dead."

SELF-DISCIPLINE
COMPASSION
RESPONSIBILITY
COURAGE
PERSEVERENCE
LOYALTY
AND
FAITH

0-382-30732